GOURMETPIZZA

MADE EASY

Everything You Need for Homemade Pizza in Minutes

Jennifer Boudinot

HOURGLASS PRESS
NEW YORK

GOURMET PIZZA MADE EASY
First published September 2010
This edition September 2011
Copyright © 2010, 2011 Hourglass Press, LLC

Text © 2010 by Jennifer Boudinot
Design © 2010 by Meyer New York
Photographs © 2010 acpsyndication.com, © 2010 IStock, Inc.

This book is a single component of the GOURMET PIZZA MADE EASY set,
and is not intended to be sold on an individual basis.

Hourglass Press, LLC
321 East Ninth Street, Suite 8, NYC NY 10003
For bulk sales please contact info@hourglasspress.com
www.hourglasspress.com
Visit us at: www.GourmetPizzaMadeEasy.com

ISBN: 978-1-935682-004

09/2012
Printed and bound in China
10 9 8 7 6 5 4 3

Please note: While this compilation of recipes has been triple-tested for taste and accuracy, total success cannot
be guaranteed. Individual results may vary, and these recipes and instructions should be considered advisory only.
The photos in this cookbook are for inspiration and in some cases do not illustrate the exact recipe. Neither the
author, publisher, manufacturer, nor distributor assume responsibility for the effectiveness of content herein,
and caution is urged when using any of recipes or instructions in this book.

GOURMETPIZZA

MADE EASY

Everything You Need for Homemade Pizza in Minutes

HOURGLASS PRESS
NEW YORK

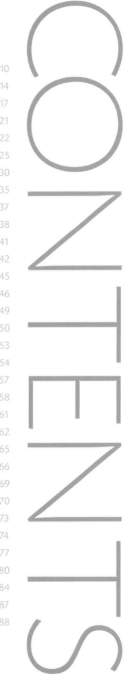

CONTENTS

Although it originated in Italy, pizza has become the most beloved food in the United States, with approximately three billion pizzas sold each year. More than a square mile of pizza is eaten by Americans each week, from $1,000 pizzas topped with caviar and lobster tail to $5 frozen pizzas from your local supermarket. The average American eats 46 slices of pizza per year, and 93 percent of the population eats pizza at least once a month (and feels sorry for that seven percent who are eating something else).

What was on the last slice of pizza you ate? Whether it was part of a gourmet pie served at a fancy restaurant, or a cold, leftover slice eaten in the middle of the night, it probably satisfied a craving for something filling and flavorful—an entire meal encompassed by a single sliver of culinary perfection.

Pizza isn't just popular because it tastes delicious—it's one of the easiest foods to eat. No forks or knives are required for this simple food, and no advanced palate, either. Pizza fits in equally well at a Super Bowl party as it does on the menu at a romantic dinner, and "pizza day" has long been the most popular for school lunch programs.

Pizza may also comprise the most varied food in our culture. Pizzerias make up 11 percent of all restaurants, and at them you can find a staggering array of original toppings. Pepe's Pizza in New Haven, Connecticut specializes in clam pizza, while Southern chain Pizza Inn offers a pizza that promises "the great taste of a bacon cheeseburger on a New York pan crust" which includes mustard and pickles. Tommaso's, the oldest pizzeria in San Francisco, offers a simple but delicious cheese-optional pizza with sauce, oregano, garlic, and basil; and Gino's East, one of the most popular purveyors of deep-dish pizza in Chicago, allows you to pick from toppings like red or green peppers, pineapple,

INTRODUCTION

and giardiniera (a relish of pickled vegetables) to add to your cheese-packed pie. Not to mention, there's always the famous fig and prosciutto pizza at Fig's in Boston.

No matter where you get your pizza, you'll always find the basic tomato sauce and cheese pie, and hopefully a tasty crust. This is the brilliance of pizza—a "plain" pie is light and scrumptious on its own, but it's also content to fade into the background of a pizza with more creative or aggressive topping choices like barbecued chicken or lumps of crabmeat. Even America's other favorite food, the hamburger, won't hold up to a topping of shrimp or truffle oil.

This quality of pizza makes your job as a pizza-maker even easier. Pizza allows you to be super creative—what you put on top is limited only by what you can find at your grocery store or farmers' market. Luckily, you don't need to be a master chef to reverse-engineer a pizza recipe. So if you find a pie

you like, buy the ingredients yourself and try making it at home. Just start with a good crust and a good sauce (both of which you can find inside this book), then let your creativity run wild.

On the following pages, you'll find lots of complete recipes, from the simple (Pizza Margherita) to the more adventurous (Butternut Squash Pizza with Fontina and Romano). Follow the recipe exactly as it is, or feel free to experiment! Making food to your taste is what cooking is all about, so if you prefer more cheese, different toppings, or a less crispy crust, it's as effortless as making a few simple modifications to the recipe to suit your style. To make it easier for you, recipes for several types of crust are included in the "Dough" section, and you can find a wide variety of sauces—from mushroom pesto to spicy tomato—throughout. Mix and match to find the one that your family raves about! Also included at the end of this book is a list of easy pizza

add-ons—toppings and other additions that you can use to create your own pizza or complement a recipe elsewhere in the book.

Before you begin making pizza, gather all your new equipment. Your pizza stone will have to preheat in the oven before you use it; never put a room-temperature stone in a hot oven. If you're making your own dough, you'll need a big mixing bowl and a large, flat area where you can roll it out in some flour. Most toppings can be prepared while your dough is rising, but it's not a bad idea to prepare your sauce first so its seasonings have time to commingle with each other. Either way, make sure you have a plan for your pie, as what you put on top can affect how much cheese and what kind of sauce you'd like to use. The easiest mistake to make is adding too many toppings—you'll find a pizza with a few well-balanced ingredients will have a better taste than one loaded with all your favorite foods (and

it will be easier to eat!). Like all kinds of cooking, making a pizza is trial and error, so if your crust isn't quite as airy as you'd like or you added too much sauce, make a note of it and try it a different way next time.

No matter how your pie turns out, you'll find that making pizzas is a fun, easy, and relatively inexpensive way to get dinner on the table, make hors d'oeuvres that impress your party guests, and even get your kids involved around the kitchen. And whether you ultimately decide to put mustard, figs, or pickled veggies on your pie (hopefully not all three!), you're sure to increase your family's pizza consumption to more than the usual 46 slices per year. So knead your dough, find some fresh tomatoes, and enjoy! The perfect pizza creation is just a page-turn away—and limited only by your imagination.

A BRIEF HISTORY OF PIZZA

It's hard to pinpoint when the modern pizza was invented, but everyone agrees on where it was invented—Naples, Italy. The residents of Naples consumed various kinds of flatbreads long before the pizza came into being. These ancient precursors to the modern pizza were usually topped with herbs and whatever else was left over in the kitchen, and for special occasions they were covered in a grated, hard cheese called caciocavallo. No one knows exactly when tomato sauce turned these flatbreads into the pizza we know today, but it must have been after 1544, when the tomato was first recorded in Italy. Brought back by explorers from the New World, tomatoes were thought to be poisonous by most Europeans. However, they thrived in Italy, and especially in Naples, where the soil—enriched with lava from Mt. Vesuvius—made tomatoes extra sweet.

For the most part, pizza was not a meal of the wealthy, but of the working poor. They bought pizza from vendors and ate it on the street (like most pizza in Italy is still consumed today) for breakfast, lunch or dinner. Perhaps it was because it was associated with the lower classes that it took pizza so long to catch on. According to the book *Pizza: A Global History*, it was treated with such disdain by visitors that Carlo Collodi, the author of *The Adventures of Pinocchio,* wrote that it looked like "the complicated filth that matches the dirt of the vendor." Samuel Morse, meanwhile, described it as "a piece of bread that has been taken, reeking, out of the sewer."

By the19th century, however, pizza had begun to be sold in restaurants that actually had tables and seats, and its popularity expanded. In 1889, it was even served to royalty, the visiting Queen Margherita of Savoy. Legend has it that this pie—with sauce, mozzarella cheese, and basil, used to mimic the colors of the Italian flag—was the first modern pizza.

It didn't take long for pizza to spread to the United States, where Italian immigrants were arriving daily. Pizza was supposedly first brought to the Americas by Gennaro Lombardi, who began selling "tomato pies" out of his New York City grocery shop in 1905. Italian workers at nearby construction sites would tell Lombardi how much they could afford (usually a couple of cents), and Lombardi would dispense as many slices as he felt the fee covered. You can still visit Lombardi's Pizza in New York's Greenwich Village, now operated by Gennaro's grandson Jerry.

Pizza exploded in popularity after World War II, and it didn't take long to spread to the corners of the Earth. Pizza can now be found just about everywhere, with plenty of regional variation. Australian pizza most often has shrimp on it, and sometimes egg. Costa Ricans eat coconut on their piz-

zas, while Russians prefer it with a paste of sardines, tuna, mackerel, and salmon. In Argentina, pizza is usually served with *fainá*, a pizza-like crust of chickpeas. Order a *mayo jaga* pizza in Japan and you'll get one with mayonnaise, potato, and bacon. In Romania, pizzas have very little cheese and sauce and are often topped with corn. Spicy pizzas in India usually include a meat from the tandoor and plenty of *paneer* (cheese curd) on top. No matter where you are, you can usually find a place to buy a pizza.

One of the most popular foods in the world today, pizza has come a long way since its humble beginnings on the streets of Naples. It's now a $30 billion industry, with a further reach than even Queen Margherita could have ever imagined. Luckily, the taste of fresh, herbed bread with tomatoes and cheese is just as tasty now as it was then.

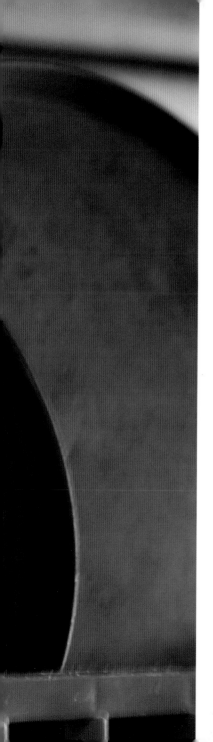

YOUR PIZZA-MAKING TOOLBOX

A wide variety of kitchen equipment is available to help you make the perfect pie in your own home. Once you've got your mixing bowls, knives, and other kitchen staples ready, here are the pizza-specific tools that make pizza night even easier.

Pizza pan. If you're making a deep-dish pizza, a deep pan is essential for giving your dough a framework for baking. Although there are pans made especially for deep-dish pizza, a pie or cake pan works just as well. Grease the pan and place it in the middle of the oven; preheating the pan is not necessary. It's also recommended that you don't use a non-stick pan, because the rigors of pizza making can cause it to nick and scratch.

Pizza screen. Even though one isn't included in this kit, many people like to use a pizza screen for an extra-crispy, more evenly cooked crust. Pizza screens are made of a wire mesh, and can be used in lieu of a peel for transporting your pie into the oven. Simply grease the screen and place it directly onto your pizza stone. You should be able to simply slide the pizza off onto your cutting surface when it's done, but if the dough gets stuck you may need to cut the pie on the screen and then pry the pieces loose.

Pizza cutters. There are a wide variety of pizza cutters available, from large, semi-circular blades called "pizza rockers" to laser cutters guaranteed to give you the perfect slice every time. Inside this kit you'll find a basic pizza wheel, which will help you easily cut the pizza into personal portions without shredding the toppings.

Spatula. I also recommend keeping your long, metal spatula on hand throughout the creation of your pie. It can be useful to separate dough from a sticky board, or to position your pizza perfectly centered on the stone in the oven. From transferring dough to ultimately serving your pizza slice by slice, you'll find your spatula is a very handy tool to have during the entire pizza-making process.

SEASONING YOUR PIZZA STONE

The stone included in this kit is made of state-of-the-art Cordierite, a recently developed material that was created especially to heat up at very high temperatures without cracking -- perfect for a pizza stone. Like any pizza stone, you should season it before you first use it and periodically throughout its life.

To season your stone, simply place the dry Cordierite stone in the center of the oven on the middle rack and heat up your oven to 500°, making sure to allow the stone to heat up with it, (you should never place it in a preheated oven). After it sits for 20 minutes, turn off the oven and let the stone cool back down. Your stone will darken and season with continued use.

Now your stone is ready to support the pizzas of your imagination, creating a crisp, crunchy bottom that is not burned. Experiment with oven temperatures between 450° and 500° to find the amount of heat that produces your ideal crust. In between pizza-making adventures, you can keep your stone in the oven even while cooking other dishes, and it won't get damaged while it sits on the rack, waiting for its next pie.

Pizza stone. Using a pizza stone is the easiest way to replicate the crispy crust of a pizza made in a professional brick oven. Leave plenty of time for the stone to heat up about 30 to 40 minutes. Pizza stones are porous, so washing them them with dish soap can make future pizza crusts taste soapy. Therefore, to clean the stone, scrape off any browned, stuck-on bits while it's still hot, then allow it to cool and wipe with a damp cloth. Although your stone will become stained over time from burned flour, oil, grease, and the like, the high temperature that it reaches will kill any germs. For best results, place the stone on the middle rack of the oven when you're cooking a pizza.

PREPARING YOUR PADDLE

Before you use your beautiful new pizza paddle, here are a few things you should know: It is made from plantation-grown carbonized Bamboo and each one is individually milled by hand.

Sometimes pizza paddles are also called "pizza peels" and this folding format peel fits easily in your cabinets or, you can hang it on a peg to decorate a wall.

Get it ready for business by seasoning it with a little oil. Using extra virgin olive oil, rub 1 tablespoon into both sides of the paddle, making sure the oil permeates the handle as well. Wipe off any excess oil with a paper towel, then let the paddle sit overnight.

To preserve the life of your peel never use a knife on it as a cutting board, and don't wash it with too much water or leave it in a sink full of water, which will warp the wood.

Pizza peel. This long-handled paddle is the perfect instrument for getting your pizza from a floured surface to a pizza stone in the oven. Generously sprinkle coarse cornmeal on the surface of the paddle before you lay your rolled-out dough onto it. This creates a "ball bearing" effect under the moist dough, and leaves a layer of air between it and the surface of the paddle so the dough can slide easily. Then, use a spatula to move the dough onto the peel. If the dough folds up around the edges, simply press them back onto the peel. Be careful the first few times you use it for transportation—it's easier than you might think to have your pizza end up on the kitchen floor. Once you get the hang of it, you'll be able to easily slide the end of the paddle under the edge of the pizza, making the pie appear to "climb" on board.

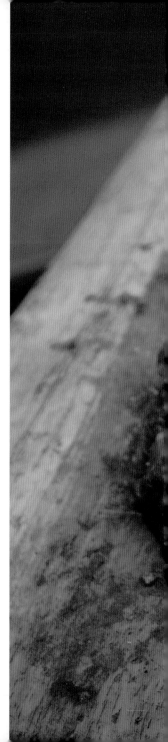

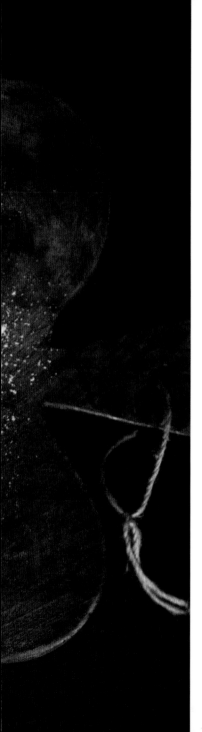

DOUGH

All good pizzas begin with a good crust. The doughs in this section taste delicious, and are relatively easy to make—as long as you don't mind a little trial and error, which is always a component of baking bread. If you're not the adventurous type, feel free to purchase ready-made dough from your local supermarket—just make sure to get the refrigerated kind, not frozen.

You may also find some of the best (and least expensive) pizza dough at your favorite pizzeria. Stop by and ask if they have any dough to spare. You'll usually find they're complimented and eager to share.

Cover grocery store or pizza-parlor dough with a plastic bag or plastic wrap and let it come to room temperature and rest for an hour or two. It will rise and become stretchy and workable, and will soon be ready to roll out to your desired width and thickness.

When the dough is relaxed and easy, line the paddle with a 12-inch long sheet of parchment paper (never wax paper). Sprinkle corn meal onto the parchment paper and drop the relaxed dough onto the sheet, then sprinkle some all-purpose flour on top. Flour up your rolling pin and begin to roll out a circular or oblong flatbread until it's thin and even, and about 10 inches in diameter. If you started with a lot of dough, you can use your pizza cutter to remove a "ring" around the edge.

After you've added the sauce, cheese, and toppings, slide the parchment paper with the pizza on top into the oven, and remove it the same way when it's done. With the remaining dough, cut 2- or 3-inch strips and fold into garlic knots! Or cut it into 6-inch squares, and assemble some smaller pizzas just like the ones served in Rome!

BASIC PIZZA DOUGH

This simple dough can be modified using the variations that follow, or used plain..

Ingredients
1 package active dry yeast
1 cup warm water
  (105° to 115° F)
1½ teaspoon salt
2 teaspoons sugar
4 cups all-purpose flour
2 tablespoons extra virgin
  olive oil

Tip

If possible, measure the temperature of the water before you use it. Water hotter than 120° will kill the yeast. If you don't have a thermometer, test the heat of the water with your finger. It should feel like a warm bath.

---

1 Stir the yeast into the water until dissolved, about 1 minute.

2 Separately, mix the flour, salt, and sugar in a large bowl.

3 If you have an electric mixer, gradually add the yeast mixture and the oil into the flour mixture while blending on low speed. Blend until the dough is firm and smooth, about 10 minutes.

4 If you do not have an electric mixer, make a "well" in the center of the dry ingredients and pour the yeast mixture and oil into it. Fold together until the dry ingredients have absorbed the wet ingredients, then knead on a floured surface, adding additional flour as necessary, until the dough is springy and smooth, about 15 to 20 minutes.

5 Divide the dough into four balls. Line two cookie sheets with parchment paper and place two balls on each. Cover with damp towels and place in a warm location until the dough has doubled in size, about 2 hours.

6 To roll the dough, dab flour on your fingers and hands and place one ball of dough onto a generously floured work surface (keep the other dough balls covered and to the side).

7 Press the dough down with the tips of your fingers, working from the center out and flattening the dough with your palms. Be careful not to overwork the dough (which will make it cardboard-dry). When the dough has doubled in width, use a floured rolling pin to roll the dough out until it's very thin. Each ball should make an 8- to 10-inch pie, but they don't necessarily have to be circular—they can be oval-shaped or square.

8 Repeat with remaining balls of dough, or wrap them individually in plastic wrap and freeze for up to two weeks.

PIZZA DOUGH VARIATIONS

Herb Crust

To give your crust extra flavor, add a teaspoon of peeled and diced garlic along with a teaspoon each of your favorite dried herbs, such as rosemary, thyme, oregano, basil.

Cornmeal Crust

Cornmeal will give your crust an interesting texture and a more pronounced flavor. To make cornmeal crust, reduce the amount of all-purpose flour to 1 cup, and add 1½ cup whole wheat flour and ⅔ cup fine yellow cornmeal.

Whole Wheat Crust

Making your pizza with a whole wheat crust is a great way to add fiber and nutrients to your meal. To prepare a whole wheat crust, decrease the amount of all-purpose flour to ½ cup and add 3 cups whole wheat flour. Also decrease the amount of olive oil to 1 tablespoon.

Gluten-Free Crust

For health reasons, more and more people are opting not to eat gluten, a mixture of two proteins that is found in wheat and other grains. Because wheat-based flour is not used, this pizza crust will have a different flavor. Gluten is also what gives dough its elasticity, so this dough won't be as firm. In order to give this gluten-free crust some help with its volume, you'll have to use xanthan gum, which can be found in health stores, specialty grocery stores, and online.

To make a gluten-free crust, use only half a packet of yeast (make sure it's gluten-free), and substitute the all-purpose flour with ¾ cup brown rice flour, ½ cup tapioca flour, 2 teaspoons xanthan gum, 2 table-spoons dry milk powder (or non-dairy creamer), and 1 teaspoon unflavored gelatin powder.

Stuffed Crust

For a cheese-filled crust, extend the edges of the dough about 3 inches farther than usual. Slice several pieces of string cheese vertically into quarters and arrange in a circle around the dough, about 3 inches in from the edge. Fold the dough over from the edges and cook as usual.

CHEESE

The most important ingredient in a pizza—after the dough and, some would argue, the sauce—is of course, the cheese. Here are some of the cheeses you'll find in this book. Make sure to experiment with your own combinations!

Mozzarella

Mozzarella is the traditional pizza cheese—so traditional, in fact, that some people don't even consider a pizza "real" without it! There are two basic kinds of mozzarella cheese: the kind that comes in vacuum-sealed package in your grocery store's cheese section; and fresh mozzarella which can either be Mozzarella di bufala (made from domesticated water buffalo milk), or Mozarella Fior di Latte, which comes from cow's milk. These can be found in the gourmet section of your store. Many people prefer the taste of fresh mozzarella, which is delicate and soft. However, commercial mozzarella is easier to shred and spread, not to mention cheaper and more convenient.

Parmesan

A classic Italian cheese, Parmesan is a natural addition to any pizza. Include it with your mozzarella cheese, grate it onto the dough before you add the sauce, or grate it over the top after your pie comes out of the oven. Similar cheeses include Asiago and Romano.

Provolone, Gouda, and Cheddar Cheese

These flavorful, semi-soft cheeses are often added as accents on specialty pizzas. They'll give your pizza a unique flavor, but should be used with care—you don't want to overpower other ingredients on top.

Fontina

Fontina cheese is a light and buttery Italian cheese that is similar to Gruyère or Beaufort. From Champagne France, only cheeses that come from the Fontina region of Italy may be labeled as such. Make a pizza with Fontina cheese and it will taste authentic, yet original.

Gorgonzola, Blue, and Goat Cheeses

Because of their texture, these cheeses must be crumbled or dolloped on top of a pizza. It will be worth the effort, however, for the rich, unmistakable flavor they add to your pie. They're so pungent that work best as one of the main ingredients—just make sure to use sparingly or you can overwhelm the dish.

Ricotta

If you like the flavor of lots of cheese on your pizza, give ricotta a try. Placed around your pie in generous drops, its super-creamy consistency will add an interesting texture to your pizza, and will balance out a pie that has a lot of non-cheese ingredients.

PIZZA

One of the best things about pizza is that it's completely customizable. Don't like tomato sauce? Use pesto instead! Found a great deal on local veggies at your market? Cook them up and throw them on your pie! Craving a filling dinner, or just a light snack? There are pizzas aplenty for you to try.

On the following pages, you'll find 20 tasty recipes for many different varieties of pizza. The important thing to remember is that it's OK to experiment! Use the listed amounts of cheese and toppings as your guide, but feel free to adjust the quantities for your tastes—whether that means loading your pizza with garlic, taking away the meat component, adding your own favorite ingredients, or any other variation you can think of. Most of all, just have fun!

PIZZA MARGHERITA

The grandmother of pizzas, the Margherita can be found all over the world. According to legend, it was first served in 1889 to Queen Margherita of Savoy. While you'll still find it called Pizza Margherita in Italy and in some American pizzerias, in the United States it's mostly known simply as "cheese pizza."

Tip

The Basic Pizza Sauce shown here is used for many of the recipes in this book. So make more than you need and freeze or refrigerate for later!

Ingredients

Basic Pizza Sauce

1 tablespoon extra virgin olive oil
2 to 3 cloves of garlic, minced
½ cup chopped Spanish onion (about 1 medium)
1 (28-ounce) can chopped or pureed tomatoes
1 cup of broth (chicken, beef, or vegetable)
2 teaspoons dried oregano
¼ teaspoon black pepper
Salt

Pizza

1 tablespoon extra virgin olive oil
1 (8-ounce) package of fresh mozzarella cheese, shredded or sliced thin
Fresh basil, about 10 medium-sized leaves, thinly sliced

Basic Pizza Sauce

1 Heat olive oil in large skillet on medium-high heat.
2 Add garlic and onion and sauté until soft, about 1 minute.
3 Add tomatoes, broth, and oregano. Cook, stirring occasionally, until reduced by half, about 15–20 minutes.
4 Add pepper and salt to taste.
5 Refrigerate unused sauce in an airtight container (will last 2–4 weeks).

Pizza

1 Preheat oven and pizza stone to 450° F.
2 Brush dough with olive oil and bake for 5 minutes.
3 Remove from oven and add sauce until covered (about ⅔ to 1 cup), cheese, and basil.
4 Cook until crust is golden brown and cheese is bubbling, about 10 minutes.

FARMERS' MARKET PIZZA

The original Neapolitan pizza on which this recipe is based is classified by the European Union as a regional specialty of Naples. So just as sparkling wine is only called "Champagne" if it's from that particular region of France, the only Italian pizzas called "Neapolitan" get their tomatoes from the base of Mt. Vesuvius. While that isn't required for this version, it's recommended that you use only the best, freshest tomatoes—so make sure to visit your local farmers' market while tomatoes are in season for a truly tasty pie.

Ingredients

2 tablespoons extra virgin olive oil, divided
5 plum tomatoes (about 1 pound), chopped
2 medium garlic cloves, thinly sliced
½ cup fresh basil leaves, sliced.
⅛ teaspoon salt
⅛ teaspoon black pepper

1 Preheat oven and pizza stone to 450° F.
2 Brush dough with olive oil.
3 Add tomatoes, garlic, and basil leaves.
4 Drizzle with remaining olive oil and bake until crust is brown, about 15 minutes.

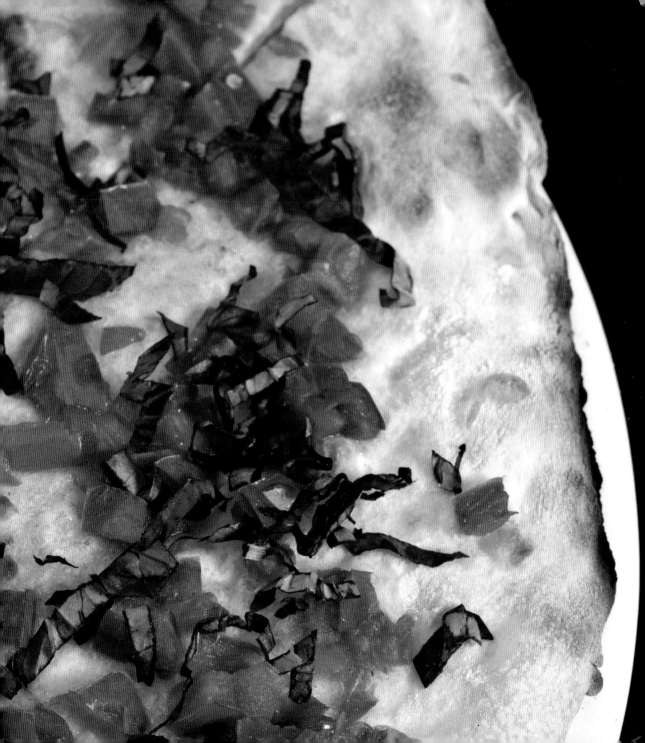

VEGGIE PIZZA

This yummy pizza is a hit with both vegetarians and omnivores alike! Because cooking times of different vegetables vary, its best to cook each veggie seperately before you add it on top. Try this pie with a cornmeal crust, and if you'd like an earthier taste, substitute some pesto sauce for the Basic Pizza Sauce. (page 37)

Ingredients

1 tablespoon olive oil
Basic Pizza Sauce (page 37)
1 cup grated mozzarella cheese
¾ cup broccoli florets, cooked
2 plum tomatos (about ⅓ pound), sliced
1 small red onion, cooked and sliced
¼ cup (about 15) black olives

1 Preheat oven and pizza stone to 450° F.
2 To prepare pesto sauce, combine basil, garlic, and pine nuts and blend in food processor until finely chopped. Gradually add olive oil until smooth and thick; mix in Parmesan cheese by hand.
3 Brush olive oil on dough and bake for 10 minutes.
4 Remove dough from oven, then spread a thin, even layer of Basic Pizza Sauce (or pesto sauce) on top.
5 Add broccoli, tomatoes, and any other vegetable you like, then the mozarella cheese.
6 Bake until crust finishes browning and toppings are warm, about 5–10 minutes.

> **Tip**
> To make this a vegan pizza, substitute soy cheese for the mozzarella.

THREE-SAUSAGE PIZZA

Sausage pizza is an American favorite, but instead of the ground sausage normally found at chain pizzerias, this pie uses sliced sausages. Experiment with different kinds of sausage to find those that suit your own unique taste!

Ingredients

Basic Pizza Sauce (page 37)
1 cup grated mozzarella cheese
1 Andouille sausage, thinly sliced
1 beef bratwurst, cooked and thinly sliced
1 chicken, turkey, or duck sausage, cooked and thinly sliced
⅓ cup finely chopped green onions
Crushed red pepper

1 Preheat oven and pizza stone to 450° F.
2 Cover dough with desired amount of pizza sauce, then top with the remainder of ingredients.
3 Bake until crust is brown and cheese is bubbling, about 15–20 minutes. Remove and sprinkle with crushed red pepper to taste.

SUN-DRIED TOMATO & GORGONZOLA PIZZA

This earthy pizza gets its bite from Gorgonzola, an Italian blue cheese, and its acidity (and a touch of sweetness) from sun-dried tomatoes. These ingredients also work well for a "white" pizza—one that has no sauce base.

Ingredients

Basic Pizza Sauce (page 37)
¾ cup grated mozzarella cheese
1 cup crumbled Gorgonzola cheese
1 cup drained and slivered sun-dried tomatoes (about 12)

1 Preheat oven and pizza stone to 450° F.
2 Brush dough with olive oil, and bake for 5 minutes.
3 Remove from oven and add desired amount of pizza sauce, cheeses, and sun-dried tomatoes.
4 Cook until crust is golden brown and cheese is melted, about 10 minutes.

> **Tip**
> Try this pizza with caramelized onions!
> (See page 52)

SEAFOOD PIZZA

If shrimp and scallops aren't enough for you, this decadent seafood pizza also includes lump crabmeat and plenty of cheese. For a spicier kick, use the Spicy Pizza Sauce on page 61.

Ingredients

2 tablespoons extra virgin olive oil
6-8 jumbo shrimp, peeled and deveined
12 bay scallops
½ cup Basic Pizza Sauce (see page 37)
½ cup chopped Spanish onion (about 1 medium)
2 cloves of garlic, minced
½ cup grated mozzarella cheese
¼ cup grated Parmesan cheese
½ of an 8-ounce container of ricotta cheese
1 (6-ounce) can of lump crabmeat, drained
½ teaspoon salt
½ teaspoon black pepper
1 cup washed and dried arugula

1 Preheat oven and pizza stone to 425° F.
2 Heat olive oil in medium skillet over medium heat. When hot, add garlic, onions, shrimp, and scallops. Cook, stirring, until shrimp are pink and scallops are opaque, about 3 minutes. Remove from heat.
3 Mix pizza sauce with mozzarella, Parmesan, and ricotta cheese and blend in crabmeat.
4 Dollop spoonfuls of seafood and sauce mixture onto the pizza and spread evenly.
5 Add the shrimp to the top of the pizza, sprinkle with salt and pepper, and cook until cheese is melted and crust is golden brown, about 20 minutes.
6 Add Arugula to the center of the pie. Continue to heat for another 5 minutes until tender.

WHITE PIZZA WITH SPINACH AND HERBS

White pizza—or pizza without any tomato sauce—is commonplace in Italy, and can be found in many gourmet pizzerias around the United States. This version uses spinach and lots of ricotta cheese. Add plum or sun-dried tomatoes if you miss their sweet, acidic taste.

Ingredients

1½ tablespoons olive oil, divided
1 tablespoon minced garlic
2 cups baby spinach leaves, chopped
1 cup grated mozzarella cheese
1 (8-ounce) container ricotta cheese
½ teaspoon dried oregano
½ teaspoon dried rosemary

1 Preheat oven and pizza stone to 450° F.
2 Add ½ tablespoon of olive oil to skillet and, when add garlic. Sauté 2 minutes until garlic is soft, then add spinach.
3 Cook until spinach begins to wilt, about 3–5 minutes. Remove from heat.
4 Brush pizza dough with remaining olive oil, then top with mozzarella cheese.
5 Add dollops of ricotta cheese and the spinach mixture.
6 Bake until the crust is brown, about 15 minutes. Remove and sprinkle on oregano and rosemary.

BARBECUE CHICKEN PIZZA

Anyone who scoffs at "gourmet" pizzas will be made a believer with this delicious gem. For this recipe, the barbecue sauce is used both as a pizza sauce and to coat the chicken. Barbecue sauce comes in many different varieties from sweet to spicy, so you may use your favorite recipe or store brand instead of the recipe below to make this pizza to your taste.

> **Tip**
> For a bigger tomato flavor, mix the barbeque sauce with some Basic Pizza Sauce (page 37).

Ingredients

Barbecue Sauce
1 tablespoon butter
½ cup chopped Spanish onion (about 1 medium)
1 clove garlic, minced
¼ cup ketchup
¼ cup broth (chicken, beef, or vegetable) or water
3 tablespoons honey
3 tablespoons Worcestershire sauce
2 tablespoons steak sauce
1 tablespoon apple cider vinegar
Dash hot pepper sauce (such as Tabasco)

Pizza
1 tablespoon extra virgin olive oil
1 boneless cooked chicken breast, cut into 1-inch cubes
¾ cup grated mozzarella cheese
½ cup grated mild cheddar cheese
1 small red onion, cooked and sliced
¼ cup fresh cilantro leaves
Black pepper

Barbecue Sauce

1 Heat butter over medium-low heat in a medium skillet. Add onions and garlic and cook, stirring, until onions become translucent, about 5 minutes.

2 Before mixture can brown, add ketchup, broth, honey, Worcestershire sauce, steak sauce, vinegar, and hot pepper sauce. Bring to a boil.

3 Reduce heat and simmer, stirring occasionally, for 20 minutes.

Pizza

1 Preheat oven and pizza stone to 450° F.

2 Coat dough with olive oil and bake for 5 minutes.

3 Coat chicken cubes with 2 tablespoons of the barbecue sauce and set aside.

4 Remove dough from oven and cover with barbecue sauce, then top with mozzarella cheese, cheddar cheese, chicken, red onion, and cilantro.

5 Bake until crust is golden brown and cheese is bubbling. Remove and sprinkle on black pepper to taste.

PIZZA WITH SWEET POTATO & CARAMELIZED ONIONS

Though they're a bit of an anomaly in the States, pizzas with potatoes can be found in lunch spots across Italy. This pie, beloved by those with a sweet tooth, will satisfy the craving without candy!

Tip

This pizza can also be prepared with white or russet potatoes for a less-sweet taste.

Ingredients

1 medium sweet potato (or yam), peeled, halved horizontally, and sliced ⅛-inch thick
4 tablespoons vegetable or canola oil, divided
¼ teaspoon salt
7 to 10 medium (1½ pounds) Spanish onions, peeled and thinly sliced
1 tablespoon butter
Basic Pizza Sauce (page 37)
¾ cup grated mozzarella cheese
¼ cup grated Parmesan cheese
2 tablespoons fresh rosemary leaves (or 2 teaspoons dried)
Black pepper

---

1 Preheat oven to 450° F.

2 Coat sweet potato slices with 1 tablespoon vegetable oil, then place in single layer on bottom of baking dish. Bake uncovered until fork-tender, about 25 minutes. Remove and preheat pizza stone.

3 To caramelize onions, toss the salt with the sliced onions and set aside. Melt the butter with the remainder of the oil in a large skillet and add the onion mixture. Cook and stir, scraping the bottom of the skillet frequently as the onions begin to brown. Cook until golden brown, about 30 to 40 minutes.

4 Cover dough with desired amount of pizza sauce, then top with cheese, roast-ed sweet potatoes, caramelized onions, and rosemary.

5 Bake until crust is brown and cheese is melted, about 15 to 20 minutes. Sprinkle with black pepper to taste.

PROSCIUTTO & ARUGULA PIZZA

This simple pizza is full of flavor! The prosciutto has a sweet, salty taste, while the with tangy arugula should taste almost peppery. Using a smoked variety of mozzarella adds a touch of smoky heartiness to this piquant pie, and you may want to use a whole-wheat crust to give it even more flavor. The key to getting this recipe right is making sure not to overcook the toppings!

Ingredients

1 tablespoon olive oil
Basic Pizza Sauce (page 37)
1 cup grated smoked mozzarella cheese
2 ounces thinly sliced prosciutto, cut into strips
1 cup chopped arugula
3 teaspoons chopped fresh thyme

1 Preheat oven and pizza stone to 450° F.
2 Brush dough with olive oil, add pizza sauce and mozzarella cheese, and bake until crust is brown and cheese is bubbling, about 15 minutes.
3 Add thyme, prosciutto, and arugula and bake until arugula leaves start to wilt, about 1 minute or less. The leaves will continue to wilt as the pizza cools.

MIDDLE EASTERN PITZA

Italy isn't the only region with pizza to brag about. In the Middle East, where the dish is most commonly spelled "pitza," delectable topping combinations combine with a thin, crispy crust for the tastiest sauceless, cheeseless pizzas you can imagine.

Tip

Ground lamb is sometimes hard to find at chain supermarkets, so try asking at a gourmet market or a local butcher shop.

Ingredients

½ pound ground lamb
1 cup finely chopped onion (about 2 medium)
1 clove garlic, minced
1 tablespoon of olive oil
1 teaspoon dried oregano
½ teaspoon ground cumin
¼ teaspoon allspice
½ teaspoon salt
4 medium plum tomatoes (about 1 pound), chopped

1 Preheat oven and pizza stone to 450° F.
2 Add garlic, oregano, cumin, allspice, and salt to lamb.
3 Add oil to skillet and brown lamb mixture over medium heat.
4 Drain off excess oil, then mix in plum tomatoes.
5 Add lamb mixture to top of pizza dough and cook until heated through, about 15 to 20 minutes.

GGPLANT, OLIVE, & PROVOLONE PIZZA

This pizza combines three traditional Italian ingredients—eggplant, olives, and provolone cheese—for an authentically Italian pie. The meatiness of the eggplant goes perfectly with the saltiness of the olives, and it's impossible to eat just one piece. You can use whatever types of olives you prefer, but for the genuine Italian experience, go with Cerignola, Frantoio, Gaeta, Leccino, or Moraiolo from your local gourmet shop.

Ingredients

- ⅓ **cup extra virgin olive oil**
- **1 garlic clove, minced**
- **1 eggplant, cut into ¾-inch-thick pieces**
- ½ **teaspoon salt**
- ½ **teaspoon black pepper**
- **Basic Pizza Sauce** (page 37)
- 1¼ **cups (about 5 ounces) provolone cheese, cut into thinly sliced strips**
- ⅛ **cup (about 20) olives, coarsely chopped**
- ½ **cup (about 6) drained and slivered sundried tomatoes**
- ¼ **cup chopped fresh parsley**

1 Preheat oven and pizza stone to 450° F.

2 Mix garlic and oil, and use 1 tablespoon to brush on pizza dough. Bake dough for 5 minutes, then remove from oven.

3 Use remaining oil mixture to coat both sides of eggplant slices. Sprinkle with salt and pepper, and grill over medium heat, turning once, until tender, about 6 to 8 minutes.

4 Cover dough with desired amount of pizza sauce, then add provolone cheese, eggplant, olives, sundried tomatoes, and parsley.

5 Bake until crust is golden brown and cheese is melted, about 10 to 15 minutes.

SWEET PEPPER & GOUDA PIZZA WITH SPICY SAUCE

With a pepper-infused sauce, and Gouda instead of mozzarella cheese, this pizza offers a completely different taste sensation than the traditional Marghertia. For a completely different look to match, try thinly slicing the Gouda rather than grating it.

Ingredients

Spicy Pizza Sauce

1 tablespoon olive oil
3 cloves of garlic, minced
¾ cup chopped Spanish onion (about 1 large)
1 tablespoon diced jalapeño pepper (about 1 small)
1 (28-ounce) can chopped or pureed tomatoes
1 cup of broth (chicken, beef, or vegetable)
2 teaspoons dried oregano
½ teaspoon chili powder
¼ teaspoon cayenne pepper
Black pepper
Salt

Pizza

1 tablespoon olive oil
1 cup smoked Gouda cheese, grated (about ½ pound)
1 red, yellow, or green bell pepper (or combination thereof), cooked and chopped
Fresh basil, thinly sliced, about 8 medium-sized leaves

Spicy Pizza Sauce

1 Heat olive oil in large skillet on medium-high heat.
2 Add garlic, onion, and jalapeño pepper and sauté until soft, about 1 minute.
3 Add tomatoes, broth, oregano, chili powder, and cayenne pepper. Cook, stirring occasionally, until reduced by half, about 15–20 minutes.
4 Add pepper and salt to taste.
5 Refrigerate unused sauce in an airtight container (will last 2–4 weeks).

Pizza

1 Preheat oven and pizza stone to 450° F.
2 Brush dough with olive oil and bake for 5 minutes.
3 Remove from oven and add desired amount of sauce, cheese, bell pepper, and basil.
4 Cook until crust is golden brown and cheese is bubbling, about 10 minutes.

MUSHROOM PIZZA WITH TRUFFLE OIL

This simple, sophisticated pie will win you accolades, even though it only takes mere minutes to make. The secret, of course, is in the sauce... or in this case, truffle oil. Most truffle oil is not made from actual truffles, which are as expensive as the finest caviar. Instead, it's made with truffle aromatics (usually synthetically produced), which are dissolved in an extra virgin olive oil base. Once you buy some truffle oil and give it a taste you'll want to use it on everything! Start with this delicious pizza.

Ingredients

2 tablespoons extra virgin olive oil, divided
¾ cup chanterelle mushrooms, thinly sliced
¾ cup crimini mushrooms, thinly sliced
¼ cup dry red wine
3 tablespoons truffle oil
1 (8-ounce) package buffalo mozzarella cheese, shredded or sliced thin
½ cup grated Parmesan cheese

1 Preheat oven and pizza stone to 425° F.
2 Add 1 tablespoon of olive oil and heat in skillet over medium-high heat. Once hot, add mushrooms and cook, stirring, until juices have evaporated, about 2 to 3 minutes.
3 Add red wine and cook until wine has evaporated and mushrooms have turned slightly darker, about 2 to 3 minutes. Remove from heat.
4 Brush remainder of olive oil onto dough and bake for 5 minutes, then remove and add mushrooms, mozzarella cheese, and Parmesan cheese.
5 Drizzle truffle oil over entire pizza and bake until crust is golden brown and cheese is bubbling, about 10 to 15 minutes.

SUPREME PIZZA

After you've tried all of the delicate pizzas with just a few toppings, make sure to try this pizza "with everything"—which you'll probably see referred to at your pizza parlor or in your supermarket's freezer section as "Supreme Pizza." This version has pepperoni, sausage, onions, and olives, but make sure to experiment with your own favorite veggies and meats to give it your personal touch.

Ingredients

Basic Pizza Sauce (page 37)
3 sweet Italian sausages (about 10 ounces)
1 cup grated mozzarella cheese
3 ounces thinly sliced pepperoni
¼ cup (about 15) black olives, coarsely chopped
1 medium Spanish onion, thinly sliced and sautéed

1 Preheat oven and pizza stone to 450° F.
2 Cook sausage in medium skillet over medium-high heat while breaking up sausage with wooden spoon until sausage is browned and cooked through, about 6–8 minutes. Drain and remove sausages from skillet.
3 Cover dough with desired amount of pizza sauce, then top with sausage and the remainder of the ingredients.
4 Bake until crust is brown and cheese is bubbling, about 15 to 20 minutes. bubbly, about 10 minutes.

Tip
Cut this pizza in two for a fun and easy way to serve! You can even roll the dough so that it is mostly rectangular.

ARTICHOKE PIZZA WITH GOAT CHEESE & FENNEL

This vegetarian pizza full of original ingredients is sure to impress. The fennel, cooked down and almost caramelized, provides the perfect counterpoint to the outspoken taste of the artichokes and goat cheese. For a variation that's great for hors d'oeuvres, make on smaller pizza crusts and prepare without the sauce.

Ingredients

- ½ **bulb fennel (white part only), thinly sliced**
- ¼ **teaspoon salt**
- 1 **teaspoon butter**
- 1 **tablespoon vegetable or canola oil**
- 1 **tablespoon extra virgin olive oil**
- **Basic Pizza Sauce** (page 37)
- ½ **cup grated mozzarella cheese**
- 1 **(14-ounce) can water-packed artichoke hearts, drained**
- 1 **teaspoon dried rosemary**
- 2½ **ounces soft ripe goat cheese (such as Montrachet)**

1 Preheat oven and pizza stone to 450° F.

2 Toss the salt with the fennel and set aside. Melt the butter with the vegetable oil in a skillet over medium heat and add the fennel mixture.

3 Cook uncovered until liquid has evaporated. Wait two minutes, then stir for an additional two minutes. Remove from heat.

4 Brush pizza crust with olive oil and bake for 5 minutes. Remove, and add desired amount of pizza sauce, mozzarella cheese, artichoke hearts, rosemary, and fennel. Add slices, crumbles, or dollops of goat cheese.

5 Bake until crust is golden brown, cheese is melted, and artichokes are heated through, about 15 minutes.

WHITE ANCHOVY & CHILIES PIZZA

Anchovies may be the most disputed pizza topping ever. Whether you love them or love any pizza topping but them, it can't be denied that they are an essential part of the pizza oeuvre. This recipe uses white anchovy fillets, rather than the canned anchovies normally found on pizza, and may just make anchovy-lovers out of doubters.

Ingredients

1 tablespoon olive oil
Basic Pizza Sauce
  (see page 37)
1 cup mozzarella cheese
8 to 12 white anchovy
  fillets that have been
  packed in oil
1 to 2 tablespoons
chopped jalapeño,
  chipotle, or green chilies
  (canned or cooked fresh)
½ cup fresh cilantro leaves

1 Preheat oven and pizza stone to 450° F.
2 Brush dough with olive oil. Bake for 5 minutes, then remove from oven.
3 Cover with desired amount of pizza sauce, then top with mozzarella cheese, anchovy fillets, chilies, and cilantro.
4 Bake until crust is golden brown and cheese is melted, about 10 to 15 minutes.

SOUTHWEST PIZZA

This zesty pizza is especially popular with kids, who love its bright colors and the familiar taste of cheddar cheese in a new setting. For a version with meat, simply add cooked chicken, or go the unconventional route and add some ground beef. Serve with a side of salsa to use for dipping crusts.

Ingredients

1 tablespoon olive oil, divided
Spicy Pizza Sauce
  (see page 61)
¾ cup grated Monterey Jack cheese
½ cup grated sharp Cheddar cheese
½ of one green bell pepper, cooked and sliced
½ of one yellow, orange, or red bell pepper, cooked and sliced
1 medium white onion, cooked and sliced

1 Preheat oven and pizza stone to 450° F.
2 Brush dough with olive oil, and bake for 5 minutes.
3 Remove from oven and add desired amount of sauce, then top with cheese, bell peppers, and onion.
4 Cook until crust is golden brown and cheese is bubbling, about 15 minutes.

PIZZA WITH MUSHROOMS, SPINACH, & SPICY SAUSAGE

This pizza takes three classic pizza toppings and puts them together for the perfect pie. If you have company coming over and you're unsure which pizza to bake, try this one! It's simple, yet sophisticated, and sure to win raves from your guests.

Ingredients

1½ tablespoons olive oil, divided
1 tablespoon minced garlic
2 cups baby spinach leaves, chopped
¾ cup crimini mushrooms, thinly sliced
Basic Pizza Sauce (page 37)
1 cup grated mozzarella cheese
1 spicy Italian or Andouille sausage, thinly sliced

1 Preheat oven and pizza stone to 450 ° F.
2 Add ½ tablespoon of olive oil to a medium sized skillet and, when warm, add garlic. Sauté 2 minutes until garlic is soft, then add mushrooms.
3 When the mushrooms begin to brown, add spinach and cook until spinach begins to wilt, about 3–5 minutes. Remove from heat.
4 Brush pizza dough with remaining olive oil, then top with sauce and mozzarella cheese.
5. Add dollops of the spinach mixture and sausage on top of the cheese.
6 Bake until crust is brown, about 15 minutes.

Tip

For a different look and a slightly different taste, add the cheese after the toppings. This method has the added benefit of helping your toppings stay in place.

BACON AND POTATO PIZZA WITH SHITAKE PESTO SAUCE

Most people think of pesto sauce as containing basil or another green. However, the word *pesto* comes from the Italian *pestare,* which simply means to pound or crush. This delicious shitake mushroom pesto topped with bacon is sure to please.

Ingredients

Pesto sauce

½ to ⅔ cup extra virgin olive oil
2 cups shitake mushrooms
2 garlic cloves
½ teaspoon black pepper
½ teaspoon salt
½ to ⅔ cup extra virgin olive oil

Pizza

1 medium russet potato, peeled, halved horizontally, and sliced ⅛-inch thick
1 tablespoon vegetable or canola oil
¾ cup grated mozzarella cheese
4 slices of bacon, sliced into pieces
½ of one (8-ounce) container ricotta cheese
1–2 teaspoons oregano

1 Preheat oven to 450° F.
2 Coat potato slices with vegetable oil, then place in single layer on bottom of baking dish. Bake uncovered until fork-tender, about 25 minutes. Remove, but do not turn off oven.
3 To prepare pesto sauce, combine mushrooms, garlic, salt, and pepper and blend in food processor until finely chopped. Gradually add olive oil until smooth and thick.
4 Brush olive oil on dough and bake for 5 minutes.
5 Remove dough from oven, then spread a thin, even layer of mushroom pesto sauce on top. (Excess sauce can be put in an airtight container, covered with additional olive oil, and refrigerated.)
6 Add mozzarella cheese, bacon, potato slices, and dollops of ricotta cheese.
7 Bake until crust is golden brown and cheese is bubbling, about 10–15 minutes. Garnish with oregano.

A PIZZA PALETTE

You've probably already realized that a pizza allows you a tremendous amount of creativity. First, there's the type of crust to use, the type of cheeses you'll cover it with, and the flavoring of the sauce (or whether you'll use sauce at all). But the biggest source or creativity comes from the toppings. Once you've decided what unique flavors you'd like to add to your pie, there are still an endless number of options for where to place them on top.

If you've ever watched a cooking show, you know that "plating"—arranging how your meal looks on the plate—can be one of the most important aspects of preparing a meal. Luckily, the variety of ingredients that you can use makes it easy to make your pizza visually pop. Here are some things to consider

when preparing your pie.

First, take a look at the toppings you plan on using. Do they display a variety, of colors and sizes? If you"dlike to use a wider array of colors, try adding simple herbs such as parsley or oregano. If you like a little spice, red pepper flakes also add both color and texture. Many toppings—especially vegetables—can be cut numerous ways. Do you want strips or cubes? Large pieces or small? Even cutting pepperoni into semicircles can add to a pizza's personality. It's also important to remember that cheese doesn't always have to be grated—slicing it thinly and strategically placing it atop your pizza can allow patches of bright sauce to be seen amongst your ingredients.

Toppings don't always have to be scattered about the pizza. If you're cooking for kids, they'll love toppings arranged into a smiley face or their name spelled out on the pie. This works especially well for small pan pizzas. Try presenting each child at a party

with their own personalized pizza for a big splash. (Adults like it, too!) If you're making a regular-sized pie, just make sure each slice will have some toppings on it—you may need to use one topping to make your design and another to fill in the extra space.

If you don't want your design to be so overt, there are plenty of other options for where to place your toppings on your pizza. Especially if your pie is rectangular, creating a "checkerboard" pattern of small groupings of toppings will make it look unique. To help guide you, use a butter knife or chopstick to lightly "draw" the grid into the sauced dough beforehand. Then place one or two ingredients in each square, alternating as you go across the pizza. You may also want to leave some squares empty so that the flavor of the sauce comes through.

If you're making a pizza with toppings for different tastes, make it clear which side of the pizza has what topping! Use more crust to divide your pie into halves or quarters. Simply take some of your dough and roll into a cylinder that has a $1/3$-inch diameter and can stretch all the way across your pie. Holding it at both ends, twist in opposite directions from both sides so that it looks like a rope, then place across your pie. When placing your toppings, leave this dough divider exposed, and you'll have a perfectly partitioned pizza.

Remember—the order in which you place the toppings on your pizza is up to you. Think carefully about whether to place the toppings before, after, or in the middle of sprinkling on the cheese. It's also important to keep the flavor of each ingredient in mind. Something with a bold taste, like goat cheese, should be used sparingly, while mellow ingredients, like tomatoes, are usually best spread all over the pie. However you decide to top your pizza, experiment and have fun! Even if your pizza palette doesn't end up looking quite how you expected, it will still taste delicious.

PARTY PIZZAS

Pizza is so popular, it's not surprising that it's also a hit at parties. For an easy dinner party, gather plenty of ingredients and allow your guest to roll their own dough and add their favorites to the top. If you're having a cocktail party, pizza makes a perfect hors d'oeuvre—especially when you use gourmet ingredients like caramelized onion, gorgonzola cheese, or truffle oil. The topping suggestions in this book should give you plenty of places for your mini pizzas to end up, but where do you begin? Following are several ways to make smaller pies that are easier to pass.

• Make a normal-sized pizza and cut it into squares. The usual long triangles of pizza are a bit unwieldy for parties, so try a more compact square size (about 1½ to 2 inches across). The up-side to this method is that it's as easy as making a pizza as you usually would, then running your pizza cutter over it in criss-crossing lines. The down-side is that if you use too many toppings, your mini pizzas can become rather messy unless you're also handing out plates.

• Use the Basic Pizza Dough recipe on page 37, but rather than dividing the dough into four balls, make twelve balls instead. Using a rolling pin, flatten each ball into a circle that is 2½ to 3 inches across. These little crusts will require some preheating, so before you add any toppings, bake them for 10 minutes in an oven preheated to 400° F. To help keep the sauce from slipping off the sides, roll the edges of each pizza up a bit before you bake them.

• Also using the Basic Pizza Dough recipe, you can roll out your dough and then use a cookie or biscuit cutter to

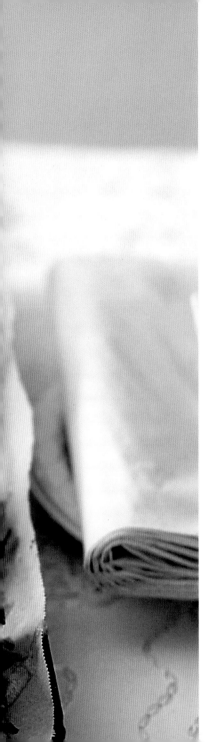

cut out smaller-sized circles to use for your crusts. If you don't have a cutter, use a cup or bowl that has an appropriately sized opening instead, pressing it into the dough and using a butter knife to help cut out the circles. Preheat the dough as above, and bake at a lower temperature than you would a normal-sized pizza. This easy method works best if you're using no sauce or a pesto sauce—and these tiny pies will also be the perfect size for placing a single slice of tomato on top.

• If you're making pizzas with tomato sauce, try using English muffins as your pizza crust. Simply cut the muffin in half lengthwise, add your toppings, and pop in the oven. The airiness of muffins allow them to soak up sauce, so you don't have to worry about it ending up on anyone's outfit. English muffins will also give you a sweeter dough, similar to a cornbread crust. Keep some shredded mozzarella and Basic Pizza Sauce on hand—these also make great after-school snacks for kids!

• Another great alternative to using pizza dough is cutting small, thick slices off of Italian bread. Add your favorite toppings, then top with plenty of shredded cheese to help keep them from sliding. If you're not using a sauce on top, first butter the bread and roast in the oven for about 5–7 minutes, until the bread is just about to brown. It's never a bad idea to add some garlic to the butter for a garlic-bread version of these delicious pizza appetizers.

• Use a refrigerated biscuit dough. Bake the dough at the temperature listed on the container, but flatten the rounds with your fingertips or a rolling pin before you bake them. These will cook up fast (in about 15 minutes), so you won't need to bake the dough before putting your toppings on.

EASY PIZZA ADD-ONS

Capers. Often used in Italian sauces and salads, these pickled buds of the caper plant are intensely flavorful, so use sparingly. You may want to sprinkle them on your pizza before you add the cheese to keep them from rolling off!

Caramelized onions. Put this sweet treat on your pizza and you'll get lots of requests for it again. To caramelize onions, toss ¼ teaspoon salt with 7 to 10 medium (1½ pounds) Spanish onions that have been peeled and thinly sliced. Melt 1 tablespoon of butter with 3 tablespoons of vegetable or canola oil in a large skillet and add the onion mixture. Cook on medium heat and stir, scraping the bottom of the skillet frequently as the onions begin to brown, about thirty to forty minutes.

Cherry tomatoes. If you like a lot of acidity on your pizza but don't want to add more sauce, slicing cherry tomatoes and including them with your toppings is a great way to get some fresh tomato flavor.

Corn. In certain parts of the world, putting corn on pizza is commonplace. You can use the fresh, canned, or frozen variety, and may want to spread it over the pizza before adding cheese. Tastes especially good on sauceless pizzas!

Garlic. If you love garlic, you'll find it's hard to put too much on your pizza. Slice peeled cloves thin and add with the rest of your toppings, or sauté in some olive oil ahead of time to make sure they're cooked through.

Olives. To add a little salt to your pizza while staying authentically Italian, add some sliced green or black olives on top.

Parmesan cheese. To give your cheese a more complex flavor, mix the standard mozzarella with grated Parmesan. You can also use Asagio or Romano cheeses. To give your pizza more texture, add shaved Parmasean cheese after the pie has been cooked and has cooled slightly.

Pineapple chunks. Some pizza purists scoff at putting fruit on their pie, but others love the sweet taste. To add pineapple chunks, simply purchase some canned in juice, drain, and throw on top! Pineapple and ham make a great combination, and pizza featuring both is often called "Hawaiian pizza."

Roasted red peppers. These sweet, cooked bell peppers are a great addition to practically any pizza. To make, roast a bell pepper (of any color) over a flame or in the broiler until blackened on all sides. Let sit in closed paper bag until cool, about

10 minutes. Peel off the blackened skin, then deseed and slice into thin strips. Red Pepper Flakes. Available in the spice aisle of your grocery store, red pepper flakes will add a bit of hotness and color to your pizza. Sprinkle on after your pie has been cooked.

Ricotta cheese. This extremely soft cheese can be found in whole-milk or part-skim varieties and is great for adding a perfect, pleasing new texture to your pie. Simply dollop spoonfuls around the pizza before baking.

Sautéed spinach. If you're looking to get some healthy vegetables on your pizza, spinach is a popular option, as it goes perfectly with cheese and tomatoes. Wash and break apart the leaves, then cook in a skillet with minced garlic and a little bit of olive oil. Don't cook for too long, however, or you'll lose vital nutrients. Once the leaves start to wilt, remove them from the heat.

METRIC EQUIVALENTS

LIQUID INGREDIENTS

Customary	Metric
1 teaspoon	5 ml
1 tablespoon	15 ml
1 cup	240 ml
1 quart (4 cups)	.95 liter

DRY INGREDIENTS (Weight)

Customary	Metric
1 ounce	28 grams
½ pound	227 grams
1 pound	454 grams

OVEN TEMPERATURE

Fahrenheit	Celsius
350°	176°
375°	190°
400°	204°
425°	218°
450°	232°
475°	241°

ACKNOWLEDGMENTS

This book is dedicated to my wonderful and creative family who participated in making and eating what seems like *thousands* of homemade pizzas over the years! I love you, Phil, Sophia and Alex and thank you for sharing the warmth of pizza together.

–KMG

Grateful acknowledgement goes to the never-ending support and friendship of many good people! Bruce, Michael, Margaret, Rage, Jeff, Joe's Dairy and Russo's in NYC, Sally and Chic, Jackie, Jen, Gabe, you have our heartfelt, garlic-breathed "Thank you, one and all!"

—Hourglass Press LLC

EDITORIAL DIRECTOR: KAREN MATSU GREENBERG

DESIGN: JACKIE MERRI MEYER
WWW.MEYERNEWYORK.COM

TEXT: JENNIFER BOUDINOT

PHOTO CREDITS:

ACP MAGAZINES
© acpsyndication.com: pages 8, 10/11, 13, 14/15, 16, 19, 24, 34, 47, 59, 63, 67, 75, 76a, 76b, 76c, 81, 82, 88.

ISTOCK.COM
© iStock Photo Agency: pages 2, 6/7, 20, 23, 27, 28, 29, 31, 32/33, 36, 39, 40, 43, 44, 48, 51, 52, 55, 56, 60, 64, 68, 71, 72, 75b, 76d, 76e, 76f, 78, 85a, 85b, 86.